VOGUE ON

CALVIN KLEIN

Natasha Fraser-Cavassoni

quadrille

Fraser-Cavassoni, Natash
Vogue on Calvin Klein /
2017.
33305240923676
cu   08/21/18

Calvin Klein poses with models including Gail Elliott and Susan Miner as he unveiled a space at London's Harvey Nichols department store in 1989.

Page 1 *Alex Chatelain captures Gail O'Neill in a classic Calvin Klein outfit of outsized navy cashmere twinset – cardigan and roll neck jumper – cream flannels with front pleat and crocodile leather sandals.*

Previous page *Naomi Campbell in Klein's signature mini slip dress, sequinned for the festive season. Photograph by Tyen.*

'IT'S AMERICAN, IT'S PURE, IT'S NOT FAKE, ARTIFICIAL, DECORATIVE.'

BARON NICOLAS DE GUNZBURG

JUST A BOY
FROM THE BRONX

The designer Calvin Klein was the master of minimalism, often referred to as the King of Clean – 'clean' describing his unfussy clothes with simple lines. 'He was the first to understand how to say more with less', wrote Eve MacSweeney for *Vogue*, noting that his clothes offered women 'practical elegance and cool, understated chic'. With an unerring ability to keep his finger on the pulse of fashion, he also channelled his imagination into wildly successful advertising campaigns and a sequence of fantastic scents, creating a multi-billion-dollar empire that included jeans and underwear. And he came to embody the American Dream: 'He put it in a bottle, he can say it in a photograph, he can do it in real life', continued MacSweeney.

There was also Klein's personal charm and charisma. Tall, dark, green-eyed and movie-star handsome, he captivated the public. His life was glamorous, daring, occasionally dramatic and even decadent. He divorced young, partied at Studio 54, admitted to his bisexuality, shocked many by marrying his studio assistant Kelly Rector, and then checked into rehab for substance abuse. Indeed, it is hard not to agree with Lisa Armstrong in her *Vogue* article, aptly called 'The Calvinist Principle', that 'every event in his life' seemed 'to acquire the status of mythology.' Yet whatever Klein did, his fans accepted him wholeheartedly and purchased everything he had to offer. They admired his mixture of honesty, directness and pride in being US born and raised. American *Vogue*'s Julia Reed described Klein as being 'a driving force behind American fashion', creating entire industries and changing the face of American advertising, and wrote that he defined a 'uniquely American style. Through it all, the clothes have never been anything less than thoroughly modern and easy and timeless.'

Model Bridget Hall displays the all-American sporty element of Klein's designs wearing his orange lycra bikini. Photograph by Regan Cameron, 2002.

Overleaf *In Calvin Klein's matelot top, wide trousers and matching slingbacks, supermodel Cindy Crawford injects glossy energy to Klein's understatement in 1987 (left). Jill Goodacre wears Klein's practical and elegant leisurewear in 1999 (right): a white cotton knit short-sleeved shirt and matching cycling shorts. Both photographs by Patrick Demarchelier.*

'This was modern dash.'

VOGUE

Klein began his business in 1968, after his childhood friend Barry Schwartz lent him $10,000. His initial speciality was coats. Under the heading of '1972 – The New Nonchalance in Fashion', American *Vogue* featured his 'no collar, no lining' design, calling it 'the coat that's a sweater'. Referring to it as 'weightless, cozy, soft as a soft white cardigan', they described it as 'something to just throw on over a shirt and pants, tie in an offhand way – and go.'

Vogue reflected the young Calvin Klein's design philosophy. He thought that 'American women needed to be more streamlined' because, in his opinion, fashion rules had changed, as had women's lifestyles. 'They moved faster, they were working, they were raising kids … they were busy – they didn't have time to change. They went to work, to the theatre, to a restaurant. That was my inspiration. What I didn't know is that there were people all over the world who were thinking the same way.' Klein's effortless designs captured the zeitgeist, as he would do throughout his career. According to Armstrong, 'luxuriously modern and covetable though his clothes are, it's his uncanny knack for empathising with the times that has made him a household name. When he lived on the wild side, so did the rest of the world. When he discovered family values, we did too. The only difference is that Klein uses his personal experiences as props in his marketing strategy.' In many ways, this personal touch showed the fearlessness and self-confidence of someone who had known that he wanted to design clothes from the tender age of five and was thoroughly encouraged by his mother.

Calvin Klein and his business partner Barry Schwartz, suitably surrounded by Vogue images in their New York office. Childhood friends, they joined forces and forged a fashion, jeans, underwear and lifestyle empire.

Born on November 19, 1942, Klein was brought up with an older brother and younger sister in a Jewish immigrant family in the northern part of the Bronx, near Riverdale. His father Leo, who was born in Budapest, owned a grocery store in Harlem. He taught his son about hard work, the significance of putting in long hours and the difference in types of customers: those who were prepared to pay an extra 20 cents for a pound of grapefruits versus those who weren't – a key lesson for the fashion business. His mother Flore, known as Flo,

on the other hand was a 'fashion freak' who set her son onto the path to the world of design. 'She loved clothes and she was very subtle about it', Klein recalled. 'She would have fur but it would be fur-lined coats. She loved neutral colours, tweeds and she would sketch.' Considering that they were a very middle-class family, her tastes were extravagant. 'Every time I get crazy about clothes I think about my mother spending all of my father's money during the war', Klein would reveal to *Vanity Fair*'s Ingrid Sischy. Flo also had a creative slant. Every few months, she would re-paint the family apartment, although this wasn't to her son's taste. 'I hated the way the place looked, I couldn't bear it', Klein admitted. Nevertheless, enjoyable afternoons were spent with her on Bainbridge Avenue where her mother Molly Stern owned a dress and alteration shop. Capable of making everything without a pattern, the skilled Molly had once worked for Hattie Carnegie, the American sportswear designer. The young Calvin would sit there sketching away while endless customers passed by. 'I spent the first ten years of my life designing in beige, cream, white, brown because those were all the colours that [my mother] loved', Klein later said.

Mike Reinhardt captures the wearable dynamism of Klein's designs in 1980 when photographing his beige covert side-buttoned trench coat; it has power shoulders, full sleeves and is camel lined.

Meanwhile, he shared money-making schemes with Barry Schwartz, who later became his business partner. Meeting when they were five, their first venture was selling cups of water, on a street corner, that they got for free from Molly's shop. And the second was selling newspapers like the *Daily News* and the *Mirror* at a mark-up. Schwartz, his best friend, always supported Klein in a neighbourhood that was fairly straight and macho. 'Most people didn't understand', remembered Klein. 'They were playing baseball and I was going to art class [at the Art Students League]… I don't think anybody thought of it as straight, gay.' However, gifted as he was – his high school, P.S. 80, commissioned him to paint a mural on its fifth floor – he was clearly different. Describing himself as 'edgy', Klein 'wanted to look like some kind of tough guy, like James Dean'. Ralph Lauren, who came from the same neighbourhood, opted for a more genteel look and, according to Klein, 'looked like he was from some other country'.

Klein was a restless child and couldn't wait to get to high school. However, once accepted, he couldn't wait to get to work. 'I was always in a rush, and I was always thinking about the next step and the future', Klein admits. His fashion-and-design education consisted of New York's High School of Industrial Arts in Manhattan and then college at FIT (Fashion Institute of Technology) where he graduated in 1963. His routine was fairly monotonous – the train to Manhattan for classes and the train back home to the Bronx, getting homework done, sleeping and beginning again. Being driven and determined, Klein didn't mind. 'I came from a family in which all they did was talk about work', he said. Fun and excitement came via the ravishingly pretty Jayne Centre, whom he had met in Junior High and who studied textile design. They began dating and then married at the Hampshire House Hotel on Central Park South in 1964. Both were creative, ambitious and keen to burst out of the Bronx and do something with their lives. However, they were extremely young. She was twenty and he was only ten months older.

Eager to earn, Klein began a stint of jobs that included illustrating for *Women's Wear Daily* and cutting dresses out of a fabric called 'whipped cream'. Neither gave much satisfaction. Indeed, Klein considered his first real job was designing coats and suits for Dan Millstein, one of the chief clothing manufacturers of New York's garment district. Millstein hired him for the division that made clothes for larger women. Klein was employed because he was capable of sketching a line-for-line copy of a garment after only one viewing and that impressed Millstein. 'At the time, the designers in Paris were setting the trends', wrote Lisa Marsh, the author of *The House of Klein*, 'and, for a price, would allow American manufacturers to send representatives to their shows.' They paid about a thousand dollars for the right to see a show or, as an alternative, agreed to buy two models for about $600 each. According to American *Vogue*'s Gerry Dryansky, 'their designers, or sketchers, as they were sometimes called, were not allowed to put pencil to paper during the shows.

Photographed for British Vogue in 1989 by Paul Lange, Elaine Irwin's all-American looks are enhanced by Klein's camel cashmere polo-neck sweater and darker camel three-quarter-length coat. As a designer, Klein was noted for his colour sense and use of subtle shades.

Overleaf *Patrick Demarchelier emphasises the clean, modern lines of Klein's silk organza duster coat, silk organza T-shirt and side-buttoned black jersey skirt worn by Alexa Singer in 1985.*

'THE CLOTHES
HAVE NEVER
BEEN ANYTHING
LESS THAN
THOROUGHLY
MODERN AND
EASY AND
TIMELESS.'

VOGUE

with a childhood friend. However, Klein wasn't sure. As a result he went to his parents for advice, something that he rarely did because he thought he 'knew it all'. Klein predicted that his mother would be dead set against the idea, but was relieved when his father said, 'you know, I never knew exactly what you studied all those years but I have a feeling if you don't see it through, even though this is a great opportunity your best friend is offering, I think you will be unhappy all your life. You have to go through with it.' Describing it as the best advice that he ever got, Klein left their apartment on 'cloud nine' and decided to forge on with fashion.

The sharpness of this boyish, single-breasted jacket, cotton vest top and cropped trousers exemplifies the androgynous appeal and elegance of Klein's tailoring. Photograph by Vincent Peters, 2002.

The Bonwit Teller order forced Klein and Schwartz to move from the cramped York Hotel to a larger but dingy space on 37th Street and Ninth. They did everything themselves, from selling to shipping. According to writers Steven Gaines and Sharon Churcher in their book *Obsession: The Life and Times of Calvin Klein*, 'they transported fabric in their own cars to save trucking fees' and 'existed on black coffee in paper cups and burgers sent in from a nearby luncheonette'. Since they often shipped at three in the morning, it meant sleeping either on the floor or the studio's convertible sofa. No detail escaped Klein's perfectionist eye. He would allow almost four days to pin, steam, shape and mould a jacket. Schwartz viewed those early years when they 'struggled so hard to ship every single coat' – even their mothers sewed on labels – as the best of times. 'We'd get phone calls from people who would reorder at full price', he recalled; this was unusual for retail.

Overleaf *Klein's early designs made an immediate and lasting impact because of their clean-cut wearability as demonstrated by this wheat knit buttoned coat dress, worn by Maudie James (left), and wheat knit fisherman's coat with hood, drawstring waist and cuffs teamed with matching knickerbockers, worn by Gunilla Lindblad (right). Photograph by Gianni Penati, 1971.*

To kick off New York's autumn selling season, Custin featured Klein's collection in Bonwit Teller's Fifth Avenue windows. She also chose Klein as the store's standing advertisement in the Sunday *New York Times*, which would be noticed by the entire fashion world. It demonstrated tremendous belief in Klein, and paved the way for his success in the Seventies.

'SIMPLICITY IS HOW IT HAS TO BE.'

CALVIN KLEIN

VOGUE

big new values
in fashion
and beauty

how to...

collect clothes that
look right everywhere

bring your looks up to date

buy now for any season

special 10-

how to get the most out of you

which skirt lengths look right now

all year beauty plan

month-by-month beauty care calendar

the best ways to color your hair

what you get for your beauty dollar

look better, feel better

what hormones can do for you

one wardrobe for all seasons:
how a great individualist does it

sun clothes you'll still love next summer

full week's food plan:
save time, money— and eat well

learn to live together for life

In January 1971 American *Vogue* showed two of Klein's designs in a fashion story called 'Wheat Knits, the Thing for Day.' 'Spring for this coat dress', they enthused, 'and live in it for the first day to the last – wheat beige knit, cut and buttoned, like a shirt to wear on its own or be over all your little dresses and pants and shirt.' They also highlighted his coat's 'sporty little hood, drawstring on waist and cuffs, all unbuttoned to show a flash of knickerbockers.'

Throughout his career, Klein has always credited *Vogue*'s Baron Nicolas de Gunzburg as being his mentor in the early years. Steeped in chic, Gunzburg's family had patronised Diaghilev and the Ballets Russes, while he socialised in the same circles as Cole Porter and Coco Chanel. Then working at American *Vogue*, Gunzburg would help develop Klein's fashion voice. 'I just worshipped him', the designer said. 'I was so thrilled that he would look at what I was doing and tell me honestly what he thought, whether it was good, not good, whether I could do better.' Their conversations stimulated Klein's vision and helped him establish the main themes that would continue in the following decades. 'He saw that I was doing something that he felt was relevant and American', said Klein. 'He kept referring to that all the time. He'd say, "It's American, it's pure, it's not fake, artificial, decorative." Not any of the stuff he disliked.'

In 1973, Klein unveiled a complete line of sportswear. It was bold, yet paid off and led to his winning his first Coty Award, the fashion world's most prestigious prize. And the following year, Klein got his first *Vogue* cover. Photographed by Francesco Scavullo, it featured Lauren Hutton wearing a 'terrific trench' that the magazine dubbed 'the coat of the year'. Inside there was a full fashion story, featuring the top model, that they described as 'part of a ten-piece collection of separates ... that is the basis for a wardrobe you can start wearing now and wear all year.' Suitably glossy with big hair and make-up, Hutton looked forceful and sensual, whether wearing Klein's 'soft shirt and slim wrap skirt' under his raincoat or 'pants and smock jacket over a soft-tie blouse of black-and-écru stripes'. Contemporary in style yet

Promoted as the coat of the year, Klein's Honan silk raincoat produced his first American Vogue cover in 1974. Worn by the actress and model Lauren Hutton, this classic trench coat epitomised the soft, practical elegance with which Klein won over a generation of American women. Photograph by Francesco Scavullo.

channelling Claire McCardell, the 1940s American designer and pioneer of the sportswear look, all Klein's clothes could be worn nowadays – thus passing the great fashion litmus test. No doubt it explained why he won the Coty Award once again in 1974.

Klein's career and business had taken off and would continue to soar. Unfortunately, his success took its toll on his marriage, which would ultimately end in divorce. Jayne and Marci were living in Forest Hills, Queens, and Klein didn't always have the time to get there. 'They were young parents from the Bronx', Marci Klein told *Vanity Fair's* Ingrid Sischy, remembering her father before he was famous. 'There were canvasses around and he was [still] painting.' Their apartment had white wood floors and white-washed walls. 'They weren't like anybody else's [parents].' Klein behaved well in the divorce; he bought an apartment and several cars for his ex-wife and daughter. But then, according to Bianca Jagger when interviewed by *Vogue*, 'generosity is probably one of Calvin's greatest attributes'.

Francesco Scavullo's photograph of Lauren Hutton shows Klein's forte as a ready-to-wear designer. Promoted as a casual-evening look, the natural-coloured soft little Honan silk jersey tank top and matching pyjama trousers were part of a versatile collection that American Vogue termed the 'basis of a wardrobe' and 'the perfect example of fashion-to-collect'.

Overleaf Klein and Schwartz in their New York design studio in 1971, surrounded by models such as Pat Cleveland (far left) and staff members.

'Clothes that are as easy and unstructured as sweaters ... the whole mood of fashion today comes through in a way that a modern woman can understand and enjoy.'

VOGUE

'IF YOU WERE AROUND IN A
HUNDRED YEARS FROM NOW AND
WANTED A DEFINITIVE PICTURE OF
THE AMERICAN LOOK IN 1975, YOU'D
STUDY CALVIN KLEIN.'

VOGUE

DISCO FEVER

In the June 1975 issue of American *Vogue*, Jill Robinson wrote an article entitled 'Feel Free To Be You'. Formed around a series of pithy paragraphs under titles such as 'Sex is better than ever', 'You can have a career and be a mother too', 'There's no difference between men and women, just conditioning', she questioned whether the myths about American women were valid. An amusing and candid piece, it captured the concerns of feminism during the 'Me Decade' of the 1970s and its consequences. 'The New Woman is, honestly, living with one foot in the past and one foot in the future which gives one no place at all in the present', Robinson opined. 'And we're having a hell of a time fitting into all this freedom that they say is going around. We seem, for one thing, to have these children.' Albeit mildly tongue-in-cheek, it did suggest that contrary to their international reputation, sophisticated American women were not living the liberated life of Reilly. Indeed, many felt confused, many felt angry, many felt guilty, but in spite of feminists 'lashing out at clothing as a symptom', to quote Robinson, fashion was an essential part of their existence.

'Clothing will always matter', Robinson wrote, defining it as women's 'most authentic creative representation'. 'Selecting things and getting ourselves up in them is the most enormously individual thing we do.' Her words echoed the attitude of *Vogue*'s affluent readers and explained the contemporary success of American high fashion.

Klein's flawless combination of buttonless smoky suede shirt wrap, cashmere crew-neck sweater, twill trousers and satin leather thong belt worn by Jean Marie McCluskey demonstrates his idea of power dressing and why his designs became a uniform for working women. Photograph by Mike Reinhardt, 1980.

Overleaf *Described as the 'The American look at its best' and 'easy and unstructured as sweaters', Klein's range included a black panne velvet dinner dress; a black silk Chinese wrap robe with taupe silk trousers matching the trim; a double-faced unlined wool coat over a black cowl-neck cashmere pullover and trouser-top skirt; and a camel's hair sweater set teamed with narrow trousers and luggage belt. Photograph by Duane Michals, 1975.*

'I've always been interested in dressing what I call the modern American woman and women around the world who really are influenced by this modern American working woman.'

CALVIN KLEIN

Into this fairly competitive arena stepped Calvin Klein: his talent and his approach arrived at the perfect moment and fashion is, after all, about timing.

'I respect women too much to ever make them look like victims', he once told *Women's Wear Daily*. Recognising this, *Vogue* recommended his designs in most issues. In their important September issue, they even wrote: 'If you were around in a hundred years from now and wanted a definitive picture of the American look in 1975, you'd study Calvin Klein: the clothes that are as easy and unstructured as sweaters, the casual turn to city dressing – the whole mood of fashion today comes through in a way that a modern woman can understand and enjoy... and even afford for a change.' High praise, but well deserved; his unlined coats, tight vests, cowl-neck pullovers and trouser-top skirts were what women wanted.

All those afternoons of hanging around his mother had rubbed off. Both she and his grandmother – opinionated, stylish women – had instilled the importance of enhancing the way women looked. His mother was a particularly strong and positive influence. When interviewed by Andy Warhol, Klein admitted that his siblings nicknamed him 'the King', suggesting that he was more than a little favoured. Yet it gave him the confidence to become a king of his world and to feel comfortable around his clients, some of whom even developed crushes on him. Not only was he chatty and charming but he was also physically attractive. In fact, success had improved his looks. His face had gone from mildly gawky to assured and chiselled. And Klein, like President Kennedy, also possessed a major requisite for succeeding in America: a terrific mane of hair.

John Bishop photographs Janice Dickinson in 1979 in Klein's smart and stylish shawl-collared satin blouse, flannel jacket and silk and wool trousers, an outfit from Vogue American Designer Original Patterns *that* Vogue *readers in Britain could recreate for themselves.*

'He really dresses a working woman
so that she can be free to work.'

VOGUE

In 1976 he had also acquired a new talent in his company; some described her as an accomplice and muse. Her name was Frances Stein and she had previously been American *Vogue*'s fashion director. Although the professional relationship would only last two and a half years, many felt that Stein – who was officially hired as his company's vice-president and director of his design studio – made a strong impact on his clothes. Sophisticated, chic and fairly outspoken, she had one of those enviable fashion careers that had started at *Harper's Bazaar*, working with the legendary Diana Vreeland. Stein was the magazine's millinery editor. Odd and antiquated as this position will now sound, it was significant and led to her befriending Halston, the American designer, who was then creating hats at Bergdorf Goodman. After working at *Glamour* magazine, she then joined Halston in the late 1960s when the designer began his business. However the world of magazines lured her back when she joined American *Vogue* in 1972.

Stein, who was in charge of Klein's licensing and accessories, had a rare talent. Armed with her discerning taste, she knew how to pull a look together with a modern sense of elegance. Later when profiled by the *New York Times* in 1982 after she had joined Chanel, Stein claimed that her background as a fashion editor had proved invaluable. 'If I had not been trained on a magazine, I never would be able to do this work', she said. 'If I had gone to a proper design school, I wouldn't understand the vast number of products with which I am involved. But I think the ability to edit is a talent that one needs today in every phase of modern life.'

Klein's relationship with Stein would end abruptly. Yet she was with the designer when he found his self-expression and started to articulate the vocabulary that is now viewed as his: sexuality, sensuality and classicism. Even if Stein wasn't with Klein for long – and the fight between her and Klein on her last day was said to have been 'a humdinger' – Ingrid Sischy considered that 'Stein keyed in to Klein's personal style, and to what was going on in his private life, and used those insights to help clarify his voice as a designer'.

Epitomising Klein's modern sensuality, Patti Hansen sports his soft tailored silk crêpe-de-Chine shirt which American Vogue termed a top 'in a knockout colour' that turns 'white lineny pants from a restaurant lunch to easy evening'. Vogue advised that it gave a whole other mood 'with a few buttons opened, with touches of gold'. Photograph by Arthur Elgort, 1976.

In Helmut Newton's 1975
photograph for American
Vogue, Lisa Taylor wears
Klein's navy and white
tiny print cotton smock
blouse with what Vogue
describes as the dégagé
charm of a neckline left
untied. The matching wrap
skirt allows her knees to
splay easily as she appraises
the bare-chested male
model. In Vogue's opinion,
the image captures 'the
whole day-and-night gamut
of summer bareness: the
clothes, the fragrances ...
the possible consequences'.

Following his divorce, Klein had become a sexy, glamorous man-about-town who courted European beauties and boasted exciting friends. There was also the slightly forbidding bachelor pad that American *Vogue* featured at the end of 1975. Curiously teamed with Marc Bohan's country residence in France under the heading of '2 Designers for Living', their styles defined the old, stuffy regime versus the new minimalism. Described as 'modern romantic', Bohan's taste encompassed exposed wooden beams, patterned wallpaper and crocheted cushions. 'Chez Bohan, nothing is haphazard, nothing left to chance', *Vogue* wrote. Klein's Manhattan abode, on the other hand, offered 'a stark-black-and-white-and-metal colour scheme' via slick furniture, hardware and accessories designed by the interior designer Joe D'Urso. Klein's black leather bedspread, complete with matching cushions, also implied that his love life was hot, happening and occasionally 'left to chance'.

When interviewed about his home, Klein might have been describing his line of clothes. 'I want things as simple and clean as possible', he told *Vogue*. 'I'm more concerned with form, shape and line than things applied. Everything I'm involved in is contemporary.' The apartment was on the 46th floor and had a breathtaking view of New York and pivoting doors that allowed big parties with as many as 200 guests. 'I love large spaces and at the same time I love privacy', Klein said; he was photographed looking tanned, with a cigarette in hand, sporting a rust-coloured silk shirt and pegged trousers. The article ended with Klein saying, 'For me, this apartment is where New York is.'

And, having become the toast of New York, Klein could make such a claim. Top models were socialising with him as well as being photographed in his clothes. In a now mythic *Vogue* shot, Helmut Newton photographed the model Lisa Taylor wearing her Calvin Klein outfit, top untied, legs splayed apart, regarding a shirtless man in tight white trousers while twirling her hair. Alexander Liberman, American *Vogue*'s former editorial director, called it 'one of the most suggestive photographs' that *Vogue* had ever published. There was also *Vogue*'s

shoot of two fresh-faced sisters, the then relatively unknown Janice and Debbie Dickinson, who were cavorting and having fun in some of his silky and unlined designs. And there was Roseanne 'Rosie' Vela, another top model, who appeared on several *Vogue* covers evoking sensuality when wearing Calvin Klein.

American *Vogue*'s May 1977 issue had Vela wearing Klein's peach silk charmeuse overblouse on the cover. Inside the designer was featured under the title 'Calvin Klein … Romance American Style'. Carrying Vela in one photograph, he resembles a glamorous athlete with a foppish mass of hair; the six-page article also included a short piece by Valorie Weaver, headed 'Calvin Klein's Secrets'. Hardly revealing, the piece merely allowed Weaver to be effusive about Klein's sportswear – 'Nothing seemed to suit the American '70s lifestyle better. And nobody did it more successfully', she wrote – and let Klein discuss his work. What's interesting is that everything he says, such as: 'The clothes I do are always a balance between the way I want to see women dressed and the way they want to dress', 'Simplicity is how it has to be' or 'You have to do something new just to survive' are dicta that he would continue to repeat throughout his career.

Klein claimed that designing for the American body, which was considerably taller and broader than the European equivalent, was simply a matter of 'not being lazy'. He admitted to doing multiple

Captured by Arthur Elgort in 1977, the in-demand bachelor designer carries American Vogue's cover girl Rosie Vela into his New York apartment. She wears a soft silk camisole under an unlined Irish linen blazer and narrow trousers that Vogue described as being 'on the top of everyone's list'.

'I love women. I'm trying to do beautiful things with them.'

CALVIN KLEIN

fittings and getting 'as involved with producing a collection' as he did with designing it, and he claimed that the second part was as important as the first. 'As long as the clothes work, as long as they're still practical – and as long as you know women will look good in them – then they have to be right', he told Weaver. She in turn described his designs as clean and classic. 'This was no colonies-imitating-the-sturdy-British-country-look; this was modern dash', she declared.

Spurred on by the idea of redefining sportswear, Klein was fighting against 'a kind of dull sameness' that he felt was carrying on in fashion. 'If I was tired of it, I sensed women had to be tired – that people wanted a change', he said. 'Once you sense that, you almost have to change … in a way it's part of your commitment in being a designer'.

In American *Vogue*'s following September issue, Klein was part of a photo shoot called 'We Like Their Style' that consisted of fashion stars such as Geoffrey Beene, Stephen Burrows, Ralph Lauren, Mary McFadden and Oscar de la Renta posing with their favourite models. In his spread, Klein pushes a luggage trolley draped with eight models, including Beverly Johnson wearing his 'cashmere serape over handkerchief linen and grey flannels'. The trolley was obviously a reference to the role of the clothing rack in his fabled Bonwit Teller début. Amongst his fellow designers, Klein looked the most buffed and fit: triceps bulged under his pale green T-shirt while his long legs were lean and graceful.

Again captured by Arthur Elgort in 1977, Rosie Vela wears a brown cotton scalloped summer scarf dress. Featured as 'Calvin Klein … Romance, American Style', the designer described his clothes as being 'a balance between the way I want to see women dressed and the way they want to dress.'

Overleaf *Klein pushes a luggage trolley with eight models, including Iman, Alva Chinn, Kirsti Moseng-Toscani, Beverly Johnson and Maaret Halinen, wearing his newest collection, which American Vogue described as turning 'the whole world of separates dressing in a new direction'. Photograph by Oliviero Toscani, 1977.*

K lein was working hard, keeping in shape and also enjoying himself. Studio 54 had just opened in April and he, along with Halston, Andy Warhol, Bianca Jagger, Diane von Furstenberg and Liza Minnelli, became ardent regulars. Just as the El Morocco nightclub had defined New York's allure in the 1950s, Steve Rubell and Ian Schrager's establishment – which managed to be both nightclub and disco – would define a wild and fabulously charged era until it closed down in February 1980.

'WHEN HE LIVED
ON THE WILD SIDE,
SO DID THE REST
OF THE WORLD.'

VOGUE

Confirming his American Dream man-about-town status, Klein steps out with fashion maven Doris Brynner, Valentino Garavani and Bianca Jagger, his date for the night, after the Italian designer's fashion show, September 1982.

Overleaf *Highlighted by Vogue as the 'essence of gilt', Klein's exotic designs capture the party spirit in 1979. They range from a bugle-beaded suede jacket over gauze trousers and suede muff, and a silk cardigan and trousers (left), to a gauze trouser suit with shawl-collared jacket, straight trousers and silk taffeta camisole (right). Both photographs by Alex Chatelain.*

Fantastic fun and a hedonist's paradise, Studio 54 became the nerve centre of New York's fashion, arts and entertainment worlds. To be part of that charmed circle it helped to be famous and rich, but being young and attractive was viewed as equally vital. To understand the Studio 54 phenomenon is to understand what New York was going through. Social barriers had melted, and creative folk were keen to carve out a career and/or name for themselves as well as party hard. As Klein later admitted, 'who wanted to be lunching with a socialite? I wanted to be part of a whole new era that got inspired by what was happening in the world.' Describing it as 'an amazing time' in Manhattan, he said he managed to meet 'everyone from all walks of life, from any part of the world' and was naturally inspired by how they looked or what they did. 'Studio 54 was our El Morocco, our Stork Club', he said.

Studio 54 led to the release that Klein felt he needed. From an early age, he had been responsible: marrying young, becoming a young father and then helping create a multi-million dollar business. It was a life laden with dedication and duty. Studio 54, on the other hand, was an escape. He could sleep with someone different every night and he could abandon himself to drugs. 'I was experimenting during that time', he told *Vanity Fair*'s Ingrid Sischy. 'We would tell each other "in South America, they always do cocaine", silly things like that.' By his own admission, he burned the candle at both ends. 'When you're young you can do that to a certain degree', he said. 'The thing is we were successful. We managed to be very high-functioning people. So that was a source of denial.' During that period, he became fast friends with Barry Diller, the powerful film executive, David Geffen, then a leading record producer, and Sandy Gallin, the manager of Dolly Parton and other top talent. Founder members of Hollywood's Velvet Mafia, all the men were openly gay and that again released something within Klein. Sexually ambiguous, clearly Klein was attracted to women but also to men. According to *Vogue*'s Maureen Orth, 'in the seventies, he was the leader of the androgynous disco brat pack who never seemed to care who knew about his wild life'. (As he later told *Playboy* in 1984, 'anyone I've wanted to be with I've had'.)

Occasionally his carefree attitude would lead to amusing consequences, such as the time that Klein was working on his first menswear collection and suggested that his creative team join him at his weekend home on Fire Island and bring along the Scottish supplier of tweed. Fire Island was and continues to be a flamboyantly gay hangout, and Klein was sharing his house with the designer Giorgio Sant' Angelo. It led to his creative team and a highly conservative Scotsman showing them the tweeds when both designers were all oiled up, wearing only charmeuse bikini briefs.

K lein felt he had to follow his impulses. As David Geffen told *Vogue*'s Lisa Armstrong, 'Calvin's an extremist. Whatever he does he does it to the maximum. When he was partying, he did that to the extreme.' Still, Bianca Jagger (who once appeared at Studio 54 on a white horse) wonders if the rumours about Klein have been exaggerated. 'Calvin was never as wild as the press made out; if he had been, how could he have worked so hard? And Calvin worked unbelievably hard.'

The atmosphere at Studio 54 was heady with a hint of danger. The music boomed, the shimmering waiters were topless and the activity in the bathrooms – either drug or sexually related – became notorious. It was a far cry from Seventh Avenue's retail demands and board meetings. Nevertheless, it was where Klein ran into his best-ever business opportunity. It was 4am and he was dancing to the disco beat when a man approached him and said, 'how would you like to put your name on jeans?' Klein was far from sober, but he understood the significance of the idea. Designer jeans were then only beginning. The socialite Gloria Vanderbilt had launched her eponymous line in 1976 and Jordache would bring out its jeans around the same time; and of course there was Lee, Wrangler and Fiorucci, the Italian brand, that offered a bum-hugging version of Levi's. Still, Klein recognised a great idea when he heard it.

On the catwalk in 1982, Klein's calf-length suede dress with lace-up camisole top and soft leather buckled belt display luxury and simplicity. Photograph by Michel Arnaud.

Overleaf *Displaying Klein's sultry 1980 colour palette, model Beverly Johnson wears Klein's evening look for* Vogue Patterns *(left) that consists of a silk satin organza coat, with copper beading, and narrowed trousers. Photograph by Alex Chatelain. Catwalk star Esmé Marshall wears a loose striped linen shift-top in warm, subtle tones (right) that shows Klein's timeless style and the easy wearability of his designs. Photograph by Michel Arnaud.*

'CLOTHES THAT EVERYONE WEARS.'

CALVIN KLEIN

The panther-like Janice Dickinson enhances Klein's apt and covetable way with designs for the American outdoors when wearing a soft and natural-looking suede jacket, a cream shirt, his signature jeans and a lizard belt. Photograph by Mike Reinhardt, 1979.

That morning, he was headed to Frankfurt for a fabric fair, but he immediately called Barry Schwartz in the small hours, on the way to the airport. 'I said, "you know there is something interesting about … designing jeans"', Klein recalled. 'I thought this could be fun … I liked the idea of reaching lots of people.' Keen to produce them at a reasonable price, he told *Vogue*'s Ron Alexander, for his article 'The Great American Jean Machine', 'I want the girls who can't afford to wear my clothes to wear my jeans'. A business arrangement was made with Carl Rosen and Puritan Fashions, his manufacturing company. Initially, Rosen was in the dress business and according to Klein 'knew nothing about jeans'. 'My favourite expression with all of them was "Trust me. Just trust me." And Carl did … [he] was a really cool guy.'

It was the first truly important deal that Schwartz made for the label and he negotiated royalties of $1 for every pair of jeans. Meanwhile, Klein pushed denim when he could. 'Jeans are not dead', he told *Vogue*, 'they're hot and sexy and still great'. Within no time, Puritan was shipping 500,000 pairs of Calvin Klein jeans per week. Naysayers had told Alexander that 'the blue-jean market was saturated and there was talk of the demise of denim'. Klein proved them wrong.

Surrounded by patterns, Klein makes adjustments to a dress on a mannequin in his workroom in 1985. As Bianca Jagger said: 'Calvin was never as wild as the press made out; if he had been, how could he have worked so hard? And Calvin worked unbelievably hard.'

K lein had the whole world in his hands or so it seemed. However, he was to experience the dark side of fame. At the beginning of 1978, his eleven-year-old daughter Marci was kidnapped. Looking utterly distraught, Klein gave a press conference with the FBI; he was living every parent's nightmare. Marci had been tricked off the school bus by a former babysitter, who had organized the scam with her half-brother and his friend. It led to Klein's dropping off the $100,000, rescuing his child and then almost getting arrested by the FBI, who initially mistook him for one of the kidnappers. It was an appalling experience, and Klein's fans and public were gripped by the near-tragedy. Fortunately, it ended well and the episode only added to the legendary drama of Calvin Klein's celebrity existence.

'HE'S BIG ON CONCEPT. ONE
COULD ALMOST SAY, CALVIN
KLEIN IS CONCEPT.'

VOGUE

A MASTER
OF MARKETING

Calvin Klein claimed that he never set out to create controversial advertising. Nor was his advertising commercial: it was conveying the message of his fashion house. As he told American *Vogue*'s Georgina Howell, 'selling the clothes isn't the point of advertising, creating the image is'. It was an innovative approach that functioned exceptionally well, gave a constant creative heartbeat to his brand and helped it grow globally. From the beginning Klein was articulate about his attitude, focused about his vision and, to quote John Fairchild, the late editor of the all-powerful *Women's Wear Daily*, 'saw the wood for the trees'. Klein crafted his advertising campaigns very carefully, and the fact that the concepts – such as turning the athlete Tom Hintnaus into a sex object to sell underwear, or using the pubescent actress Brooke Shields to advertise jeans – were so trailblazing was no accident.

Klein's first underwear advertising campaign caused a sensation when this billboard hit Times Square in 1982. It starred Tom Hintnaus, and no one could get over the display of the Brazilian pole-vaulter's well-packed briefs. Photographed by Bruce Weber, the unforgettable image was cited as one of the '10 pictures that changed America' by American Photographer *magazine.*

Few can forget his first venture – the Calvin Klein Jeans TV commercials starring Shields – because it was scandalous, groundbreaking and effective. Directed by Richard Avedon in 1980, the 15-year-old Shields looked directly into the camera and asked: 'You want to know what comes between me and my Calvins? Nothing.' She is still strongly associated with the Calvin Klein jeans campaign and over 35 years later people still mention the ads to the American actress.

She was sensationally beautiful – a *femme-enfant* marvel – and the series of ads, which also had her reciting a monologue about genes as well as stating that she was 'Calvinized', were suggestive, playing on the fact that she was too young – forbidden fruit, but oh so tempting. The response to the ads was incredible. The billboard in Times Square stopped traffic and infuriated women's rights groups. Meanwhile, Calvin Klein jeans became a denim juggernaut.

Klein had worked closely and intensively with Avedon as he always would with photographers and directors. 'I just felt this passion', he told *Women's Wear Daily*. 'I knew what I wanted to say. I had to find the right people to help me to convey that message.'

'SELLING THE
CLOTHES ISN'T
THE POINT OF
ADVERTISING,
CREATING THE
IMAGE IS.'

CALVIN KLEIN

*Brooke Shields photographed
at her mother's ranch by
Bruce Weber in 1990. Despite
her successful career as an
actress, she is still just as
famous for her set of Calvin
Klein jeans advertisements.
Here she wears Klein's long
cotton jersey T-shirt.*

Avedon had introduced him to the writer Doon Arbus, the daughter of the photographer Diane Arbus. This resulted in 'a lot of drinking and staying up very late and deciding who the cinematographer should be', Klein recalled. Nevertheless, almost everything had been the designer's idea, from the choice of Shields's loose charmeuse shirt, which the designer termed as 'the colour of liquid', to deciding to advertise on television. Indeed, from the 1980s, Klein would become a master of marketing. To quote *Vogue*'s Eve MacSweeney, 'He's big on concept. One could almost say, Calvin Klein is concept'.

A dynamic 6ft 1in force of nature, he was also utterly at ease with his sexual magnetism, tapping into it for his brand and skilfully using it throughout his career. Journalists meeting Klein tended to be seduced. 'Calvin Klein is a taut fusion of focused energy and old-fashioned courtesy', wrote *Vogue*'s Lisa Armstrong. 'Above his denim shirt and checked jacket, the face is tanned and the gestures expansive, even if the sea-blue eyes – the same blue that surrounds the house in the Hamptons – have a habit of locking you with the unsettling intensity of the myopic or the visionary.' The charm wasn't disingenuous: Klein admired women, encouraged their strengths, and they felt it.

Actress Lisa Bonet dancing in Klein's strapless lace scalloped dress. The movement demonstrates the sensual easiness of the designer's clothes. Photographed by Patrick Demarchelier, 1987.

In his studio, he played the role of a charismatic uncle-like figure – ever curious but never quite satisfied – that his employees aspired to please. 'We were all in love with Calvin', said John Calcagno, who worked in Klein's creative studio during the Seventies and Eighties. Recalling the designer's dress sense, he mentions the teaming of a T-shirt with 'heavy tweed suits', the 'length and slouchiness' of Calvin's body, the choice of thick socks with heavy shoes 'because I think he had skinny ankles' and 'the perfection of the way the jeans sat on his body, the way he looked at himself in the mirror and adjusted them', as well as 'the oh-so-perfect T-shirts that he bought by the hundreds'. Klein encouraged creative thinking and stimulated imagination by linking colours with imagery: white became 'chalk' or 'Dover' after the white cliffs of Dover; beige was 'sand'; and black was 'coal'.

Instinctively, Klein knew exactly who could work for him and pursued them in an unabashed manner. In the 1990s when looking for a new company president to spark up and globalise his label's image, he went after Gabriella Forte, who had worked beside Giorgio Armani for decades. Unable to reach her directly, he stalked her, waited outside her house in Milan and persuaded her to join him. A prince of persuasion, if he went after someone, he was hard to resist. He also discovered talent. The future style icon Carolyn Bessette Kennedy was a lowly employee in Boston's Calvin Klein boutique before being plucked from obscurity to become a publicist in charge of the New York office's celebrity clients in the mid-90s. Described by *Vogue*'s Anna Wintour as 'beautiful and stylish in a completely modern way', it had been Klein who had paved the way for Bessette Kennedy's entrance into rarefied fashion circles.

Demonstrating Klein's timeless simplicity, Andie MacDowell strolls on deck wearing a long-sleeved white cotton sweater dress and cardigan, perfect clothes to travel in. Photograph by Alex Chatelain, 1982.

D uring the controversy surrounding the Brooke Shields ads, Marit Lieberson profiled Klein for the September issue of British *Vogue* in 1980. In his first interview for the magazine he came across as both accessible and intelligent. When asked if his American customers needed style dictates, he answered that they were 'more independent than that …When I first started to design mid-calf clothes, I'd come across women who would say, "I really love this dress but I'm afraid that I'm not going to wear it this length because I think it's going to look ugly on me. I'm going to shorten it."'

'My style, which is about purity and simplicity and less is more, has appeal all over the world.'

CALVIN KLEIN

Asked about his chief source of inspiration, once again Klein named Claire McCardell, who was designing sportswear in the Forties while her fashion contemporaries were so stiff and formal. According to Lieberson, 'the same easy feeling runs through Klein's collections, through everything from sweaters to silk, suede to slacks, natural fibres, wrapping, folding, gently falling shapes, comfortable clothes which strike the uninitiated as disarmingly simple, and to the devotee become a lifestyle. He really dresses a working woman so that she can be free to work.' Varying in style, his working women designs could range, in the summer months, from a long white linen dress to a slinky unlined skirt suit, and, in the winter, could be seen in a wool tapered trouser suit under a roomy coat or a high-collared knit and swirling plaid skirt under a blanket-striped shawl.

Describing his own designs as 'quiet, sexy and modern', Klein's clothes suited any occasion. Here Andie MacDowell enjoys the safari life wearing his cotton knitted lace-up top. Photograph by Albert Watson, 1982.

Overleaf Klein's sporty simplicity is illustrated by Elizabetta Ramella in a striped knitted sweater and striped skirt (left); the stripes are diagonally opposed yet work owing to the easy, non-structured style. Klein's handkerchief linen wrapped shirt and skirt are perfect when Ramella lunches out (right). Both outfits photographed in Venice by Barry Lategan, 1983.

When questioned if he wanted to do films, Klein replied that he had been thinking about that. 'Dressing them?' asked Lieberson. Actually, Klein meant making them. 'But I would never have the time', he stated. Proving, thought Lieberson, that he was 'a young man with a head on his shoulders', Klein swiftly pointed out that Hollywood types didn't need him. 'If they want my clothes, they buy them from the stores', he said. Still, he did reveal that he was friendly with the actress Ali MacGraw, the style muse who began in fashion and then starred in the film *Love Story*. He also admired the style of Faye Dunaway, another cinematic beauty, who had won an Oscar for her role in *Network*. 'She was strong, sexy, a lot of things that are exciting', he said. Predicting a much deeper recession in the Eighties than anyone expected, Klein was concerned by price. 'More than I've ever been', he told Lieberson. 'It's got to be quality. With this kind of inflation, women can't spend a great deal of money on clothes, so it has to be something that they can wear over a period of time, that's not going to become obsolete in a year or two.'

'CALVIN KLEIN ... ROMANCE AMERICAN STYLE.'

VOGUE

Vogue describes Klein as bringing back 'the dressier suit of the evening' when designing a ballerina-skirted dinner suit made of dark navy silk faille, worn by Lindsey Thurlow. Klein is at his best when using a crisp, natural fabric, and his ankle-length skirt is both feminine and romantic. Photograph by Peter Lindbergh, 1984.

Klein's British *Vogue* portrait – making him look casual and windswept – was by the American photographer Bruce Weber. They began working together in 1981 and would join forces for over three decades. Weber's aesthetic – making young men look Adonis-like yet wholesome and doing the female equivalent for women – became key to Klein's next commercial and flourishing venture: underwear. Weber's portrait for the first men's campaign remains unforgettable.

Using the spectacularly handsome and well-endowed Tom Hintnaus, the Brazilian-born champion pole vaulter, Weber had him arching his naked torso against a white wall wearing Calvin Klein's Y-fronts. Photographed on the Greek island of Santorini, the picture is sexy, direct and in some ways reminiscent of the stark images of Leni Riefenstahl, the photographer who glamorised the Third Reich. Klein was thrilled with the photograph and it was chosen for billboards and bus-shelter posters across major American cities. On first seeing the advertisement in New York, the writer Ingrid Sischy swivelled her head to get a better look at the poster that she described as 'basically shoving the man's physicality down the audience's throat'.

White was a favoured colour for Klein's classic, timeless designs; here the semi-transparency of the material gives this over-sized, silk organza shirt, worn by Michelle Eabry, a subtle sensuality. Photograph by Hans Feurer, 1985.

Inciting the right impulse and retail reaction – a kind of 'buy these and it will enhance your bulge' – it was the start of the underwear range's stupendous sales. Klein had added yet another domain to his empire – so much so that it's hard not to agree with *Women's Wear Daily*'s Bridget Foley that 'along with his mastery of the runway, Klein's legacy is inseparable from jeans and underwear'. 'His success at elevating such proletarian categories to the level of cocktail party conversations via brilliant marketing remains unparalleled', she wrote. 'Klein was one of the first to grasp that fashion is far less about a price point than a finely honed and, yes, calculated point of view.'

Klein's line of intimate apparel for men was launched in 1982 and to quote *Vogue* was 'a phenomenal success'. Unfussily designed, it was cotton, comfortable and also religiously worn by the designer. True, Klein tried out 'other people's underwear' but only 'to check

out the competition'. Two years later, he decided to promote intimate apparel for women. Or, rather, it had been the idea of Kelly Rector, an assistant in his studio.

When interviewed by *Vogue*, Klein said, 'it's almost like a woman wearing her husband's-boyfriend's-lover's underwear. There's something very seductive about that.' Since the line would include tanks, briefs and boxer shorts, Klein viewed it as 'a new attitude about women's underwear', offering that he was 'not someone to do ruffles and lace'. 'It had to relate to what I think is modern, young and sexy', he said. And previewers evidently agreed since they ordered a quarter of a million dollars or more of the underwear while '$18 – 20 million in business was projected for the first year'. *Vogue* described the new collection as being 'closer to men's locker room than boudoir' and noted that female customers were so won over that they began discussing 'not just about what they can put the pieces under – but where they can wear them out'.

In Vogue's 'Night Shifts' fashion feature, Carré Otis wears Klein's pale lemon underwired satin bra. The design is slightly retro in feel, and Klein added to its appeal by modernising the proportions and softening the cup. Photograph by Hans Feurer, 1989.

Twelve years later, tying in with the launch of Klein's new playtime collection of cotton pants and bras, American *Vogue*'s Vanessa Friedman wrote an article – aptly called 'A Brief Evolution' – chronicling Klein's continued success in the world of intimate apparel. 'In a market filled with other designers (Donna Karan, Valentino, Christian Dior, Yves Saint Laurent, and now, Gianfranco Ferré) how does Klein keep getting it so blooming right?' she asked. She sensed it was 'consistency'. Klein, on the other hand, said, 'what's sexy doesn't necessarily have to do with decoration, but with shape and with the unexpected: things that are masculine, childish'. 'I like the idea of putting a woman in something that could be worn by a little boy', he said.

Klein was recognising a trend – channelling one's childhood – that Friedman expressed as an adult's 'much-documented longing to return to more carefree times, when sex did not require planning or permission'. 'Which is logical, given the fact that Calvin Klein – and Calvin Klein's underwear in particular – has never been about safety and security', she wrote. 'From the immense Adonis in white cotton briefs sunning himself on the billboard over Times Square to

Kate Moss wrapped suggestively around Marky Mark and Michael Bergin on posters everywhere. Klein's ad campaigns have consistently linked sex and underwear frankly and non-judgementally.' According to Richard Martin, the then curator of the Costume Institute at the Metropolitan Museum of Art, what Klein had done for underwear was overtly 'to promote the erotic aspect' and to adhere to the modernist design concept of form following function. 'He has achieved a perfect melding of the design objectives of the Bauhaus and the marketing objectives of sensuality', Martin said.

I n many ways, Klein also added an 'erotic aspect' to the fragrance industry when he introduced Obsession in 1985. Weber took the initial photograph of the model Josie Borain and also directed the film that showed arms, hands and other body parts all over her. 'You didn't know if they were men or women', said Klein. 'You didn't know how many of them they were. But it got your mind going.' It also indicated a lot about Klein's life at the time. 'That was a period of time when sex was everywhere, as were drugs', the designer said. 'Not for everyone, of course. I've experienced – and I've said it before – a lot of my fantasies.'

Calvin Klein surrounded by American models, including Suzanne Lanza and Bonnie Berman, wearing his new line of women's underwear. Inspired by the male brief/ Y-front and an instant hit, it was more locker-room in style than boudoir.

Josie Borain was an interesting choice because although she was elegant, she wasn't classically pretty, something that was often thought necessary for the American market. Still, Klein was determined to use her. 'I was obsessed', he said. 'She was such an interesting woman and not an obvious sexpot, androgynous in a way but so fine and classy.' As for the fragrance's name, it reminded Klein of himself and his friends who were 'obsessed with work or success'. Explaining how he managed to choose a name that so well reflected the times, Klein put it down to 'a gift', that helped him zero in on the right name or image capturing the zeitgeist. 'I get an emotional reaction', he told American *Vogue*.

'Klein's legacy is inseparable from
jeans and underwear.'

WOMEN'S WEAR DAILY

'IT'S ALMOST LIKE A WOMAN WEARING HER HUSBAND'S-BOYFRIEND'S-LOVER'S UNDERWEAR. THERE'S SOMETHING VERY SEDUCTIVE ABOUT THAT.'

CALVIN KLEIN

Model and actress Carey Lowell wears Klein's striped silk slide top and matching boxer shorts for Vogue's 'The Other Evening' fashion feature photographed by Arthur Elgort in 1981. The look epitomised Klein's deft way at sensualising basic classics via his choice of colour and fabric.

'How do I know this photograph or this ad is gonna be good? Because my heart starts racing.' According to *Vogue*'s Lisa Armstrong, one of Weber's shots for Obsession showing 'three naked bodies of ambiguous gender writhing on a sofa' so scandalised the US at the time 'that the normally blasé *New York Times* banned it'. 'While the introduction of the jeans catapulted him from a $25 million to a $180 million company in one year', she wrote. 'Obsession, aptly code-named Climax, promptly broke all records at the counter.' Within four years, Obsession's sales went over the $100 million mark.

Hans Feurer photographs Kara Young in 1988 wearing Klein's olive and saffron silk satin coat with wide shawl collar and chocolate charmeuse slip for 'Free Spirit', a Vogue fashion feature. While Klein typically used classic colours in his designs, when stepping outside those parameters he achieved stunning results.

Yet in the late 1980s, Klein told Georgina Howell that designers had 'to be more sensitive about sensuality'. 'A provocative commercial isn't a shock if it's seen alongside the soaps, where the women are in bed the whole time', he said. 'On the other hand, it might offend if it came right after the news.' America had changed. The Reagan administration had ushered in more conservative times. And Klein adapted. In his designs, his choice of fabric became dressier and his clothes became more formal in style – even a little Parisian, ranging from a sharp curvy white suit to a stripy boat top matched with a lipstick-red full taffeta skirt, to long, lined lacey dresses.

Klein started wearing suits again. At Andy Warhol's memorial in 1987, he resembled a handsome senator. And when sporting his black tie at the Council of Fashion Designers of America Fashion Awards (CFDA), he brought to mind a character from F. Scott Fitzgerald – and his new wife, Kelly, in her strapless gown and opera gloves looked suitably grown-up and groomed.

To the surprise of many, or rather those who remembered his Studio 54 days, Klein had married Kelly Rector, his studio assistant in 1986. In the early years of their marriage, they would become the unofficial king and queen of New York. To considerable media fanfare, he would buy her the Duchess of Windsor's pearl necklace and eternity diamond ring. (Some thought this a little strange, given the rumoured anti-Semitism of the royal style icon and Klein's pride in his Jewish origins.) Park Avenue ladies who lunched and other socialites were also attending his fashion shows. In many ways, it was as if Klein had decided on a dramatically new existence that meant cutting a swathe through high society, though this was an odd idea, considering that he had often seemed a bohemian at heart.

But the adoption of a new, more conservative lifestyle was emerging in the wake of the HIV epidemic. AIDS had hit the fashion and arts world hard. 'Calvin lost a lot of friends from those times ... Halston, Giorgio di Sant' Angelo ...', said Bernadine Morris, the former *New York Times* journalist. 'The eighties were a scary time for him.' As it was elsewhere. Indeed, to quote *Vogue*'s Lisa Armstrong, 'by 1986, the party was over and a national hangover had set in'. There were reports that Klein himself had AIDS. He officially denied such claims in 1983, trying to scotch rumours that would be bad for business. Klein, like many others, then began to pump up his body, as if proving that he was lean but also mean – and healthy. Still, it was under these strained circumstances that he launched his next perfume, Eternity, which was named after his wife's Duchess of Windsor ring.

Just as Obsession had caught the hedonistic pulse of the time, Eternity appealed to baby boomers and promised a return to wholesome values. Christy Turlington was the face of the fragrance and Bruce Weber photographed the exquisite black-and-white images. It was Kelly who had suggested Turlington. Of all the supermodels, she was the most credible in the role of young mother and wife and the most classically beautiful. 'I always felt that her intelligence came through in the photographs', said Klein. 'At the time, there was a lot of vulgarity and that didn't interest me.' Indeed, it was thought that Eternity represented Klein and Kelly. 'The Eternity fragrance was about this ladylike setting', recalled Turlington. '"Puritanical" wouldn't quite be the right word, but very serene. It was a new life for Calvin.'

When going through his short-lived Parisian stage, Klein still managed to add a modern edge, as shown in this catwalk look: a striped off-the-shoulder top and stiff red silk skirt with a black-and-white broderie anglaise petticoat underneath. Photograph by Michel Arnaud, 1987.

Overleaf *Though Klein was the master of understatement, he was also successful when aiming for dramatic, showstopper gowns of classic simplicity. Patrick Demarchelier photographs Bonnie Berman (left) in Klein's statuesque dress that Vogue dubbed 'Cashmere taken to the extremes', being 'marvellously black, long, fitted, with a sequinned edge'. Karen Alexander strikes a pose (right) wearing Klein's white silk satin mermaid dress with a flowing train. Photograph by Herb Ritts, 1988.*

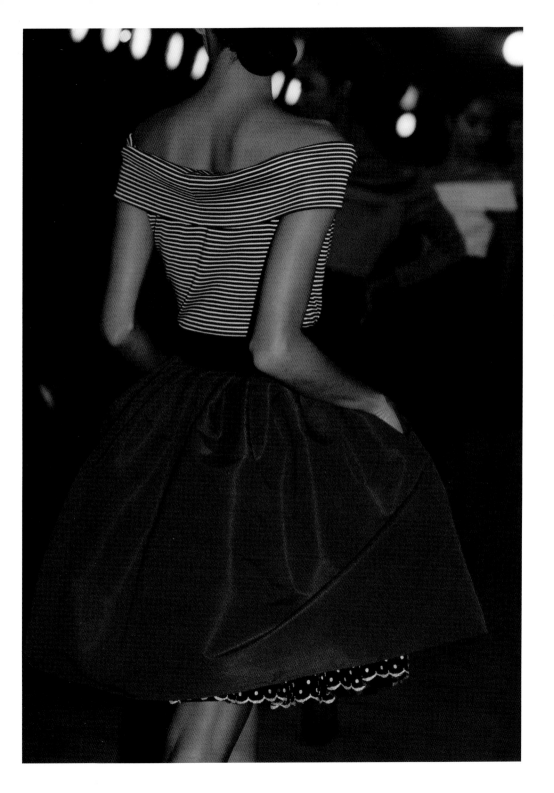

'WHEN HE DISCOVERED FAMILY
VALUES, WE DID TOO.'

VOGUE

WHEN CALVIN
MET KELLY

Throughout Calvin Klein's brilliant career, it was as if opposing forces were raging within him. On the one hand, he was extremely thoughtful as a designer, concerned about how his customers would wear his clothes. Then there was the advertising *agent provocateur* whose vision and determination set out to astonish and shock. The balance between the two would work sensationally well.

And this was demonstrated in 1985: in the same year that he launched his fragrance Obsession, he was also part of *Vogue*'s symposium: 'Is Fashion Working for Women?' Eloquent as ever, Klein declared that there were clothes that were appropriate 'for a certain time' and others that were not. 'A woman on Wall Street doesn't want to sit in a boardroom and have everyone notice her dress', he said. 'She wants to fit in, look attractive … But it shouldn't take away from her intelligence.' This obviously contrasted with the spirit of the Obsession ad campaign that showed Josie Borain being manhandled and youthful nude bodies writhing on top of each other. This was all part of Klein's package – sensible when he should be and saucy when he wanted to cause a stir.

In his personal life, there was the same dichotomy. He and his beautiful wife Kelly had married at the American Embassy in Rome thanks to the help of his friend Nancy Reagan, wife of the then President. Photographs showed a very correct, *comme il faut* occasion. This contrasted with the alarming – and contemporaneous – tales of

In 1991, Snowdon photographed a Vogue feature entitled 'From Eternity to Here', featuring Calvin and Kelly Klein at their beach house in the Hamptons. Both look perfectly relaxed and happy, she in the designer's cashmere knit jumper with matching leggings, and he in a tweed jacket over his denim shirt and jeans.

'Kelly seemed to be the catalyst Klein needed to make him look at the business and life from a fresh perspective.'

VOGUE

Klein being drunk, abusive and out of control in his design studio. On the one hand there was the elegant charmer who had a young wife, spent hours in the gym and paid attention to his diet. On the other, the designer who in 1988 checked into Hazelden, a treatment centre in Minnesota, to sort out his addiction to vodka and Valium. Klein was honest about the gruelling experience. In a revealing American *Vogue* article called 'A Star is Reborn', which featured portraits of himself and Kelly by Irving Penn, the magazine's top photographer, he opened up to Maureen Orth. Described as 'pink cheeked, blue jeaned and sitting in the nearly empty living room of his new town house on the upper east side', he marvelled about being 'reborn', 'seeing things differently' and being in the 'first year' of his 'second life.' Thanks to Hazelden's methods, he aimed to release all of his old tension: 'the terrible anger', envy and self-doubt. 'It's not an easy place', Klein said, 'but it's the best thing I've ever done in my life. I've had a terrible problem with Valium for years. The quality of my sleep is much better – I feel like a different person.' For a week, his wife joined him for family therapy.

A relaxed Klein seemed to be finally coming to terms with the idea that the universe didn't rest on his shoulders. 'Everything doesn't always have to be the way I think it should be', he said, confessing that his desire to control was tougher to shake than his substance abuse. 'I'll be working on that for the rest of my life', he said, 'that's a real problem of mine. I like to be in control. But it can be terribly frustrating.'

David Bailey photographs Christy Turlington in 1987, wearing one of Klein's best winter looks. A winning contrast of sombre and loud, it consists of a sporty wool roll-neck and high-waist grey jersey skirt worn under his plaid cashmere wrap coat that Vogue describes as 'full swing, unstructured', appropriate for wearing 'in-between seasons instead of a jacket'.

Overleaf *Viewed as one of the great fashion couples, the glamorous Mr and Mrs Calvin Klein face the flashbulbs at an AIDS benefit in 1990. Kelly's choice of clutch emphasizes the metallic glow of her Calvin Klein cocktail dress.*

'I'd always seen Christy as the epitome of the woman who was my woman – the woman who I wanted to dress.'

CALVIN KLEIN

'SHE IS SO CALVIN, THE IMAGE OF WHAT CALVIN LOVES – AMERICAN AND CLEAN AND KIND AND BEAUTIFUL.'

DIANE VON FURSTENBERG

'WHAT WE'RE DOING IS FUN — IF YOU HAVE ANY SENSE OF HUMOUR AT ALL!'

CALVIN KLEIN

Photographed by Arthur Elgort in 1991 amidst Masai tribespeople in the Tarangire National Park, Tanzania, Christy Turlington shines wearing Klein's golden sequinned evening dress. Turlington, one of Klein's favourite models, was also the face of his best-selling Eternity perfume.

Naturally, his new thinking would manifest itself in his following spring collection. 'Now I'm thinking about easier clothes, looser construction – not a lot of padding … Just more natural', he admitted. The show was colourful, with a Gauguin-inspired palette, yet quite sober and mature. Supermodels such as Iman and Gail Elliott appeared in long flowing gowns while Linda Evangelista graced the catwalk in an elegant hot pink velvet skirt emphasised by a dark blouse.

Wearing Klein's catsuit/bodystocking, Kelly Klein poses for Snowdon in the entrance hall of their East Hampton home. The picture gives a sense of the couple's eclectic decoration style: the deckchairs are chenille Aubusson, the wide dark-stained floorboards were sourced from a chapel in the American south.

Overleaf *For Vogue's fashion feature 'New Shades of Modern', Herb Ritts focused on the sculpted form and 'twist in the tail' of Klein's mermaid skirt. Described by Vogue as a 'Fishtail skirt in (the) brightest fuchsia double-face wool', it was teamed with Klein's black jersey body and narrow knotted leather belt.*

Klein's shift in his vision would also go hand-in-hand with Eternity, his new 'clean, floral, romantic', perfume with an ad campaign that was based on himself and Kelly Rector and even flaunted a baby in the background. 'I don't think the thing is to be provocative anymore', he said. 'I've done everything I could do in a provocative sense without being arrested.' Kelly would be a key element of his new life. 'I didn't think another relationship was possible', he said. 'Because of the health crisis that's going on now, people are so much more conscious of the fact that you can't go fooling around. You start questioning – "who has this person been with?" and saying, "I'm going to be more careful before I get involved." Your values change! It didn't happen, bang! I fell in love over a long period of time.'

Kelly was born in 1957. *Vogue*'s Lisa Armstrong wrote that she was 'brought up in Westport, Connecticut – the ideal WASP-y counterpart to Klein's Jewish Bronx background' – and arrived in the Calvin Klein studio as a design assistant from Ralph Lauren in 1981. A mutual friend suggested that Klein take her on. After meeting her, he called her the following morning – at 6am, no less – and told her she was hired.

'Every element of their lifestyle
is a vital marketing tool.'

VOGUE

'PRACTICAL ELEGANCE AND COOL, UNDERSTATED CHIC.'

VOGUE

Kelly's upbringing had given her a sense of style; her mother Gloria List owned a folk- and Indian-art gallery in California while her father Tully Rector was a director of TV commercials and an accomplished horseman. Kelly was also a talented rider. She regularly competed in the Class A Amateur Owner Hunter circuit and her lifestyle would be a key element in her relationship with Klein, fifteen years her senior. 'I'm disciplined', she told *Vogue*. 'Maybe it's the fact that I ride and had my training in fashion.'

Kelly was a sporty, all-American beauty. 'One word (in big, black letters) springs to mind', wrote *Vogue*'s Eve MacSweeney, 'GLOSSY, with her dazzling chestnut mane and startling, liquid blue eyes'. In the Klein studio, Kelly quickly became known as 'the skin girl' because the designer would hold fabric against her wrist to test colour. And soon she began to have influence. She wasn't a perfect model size, but she possessed natural style and knew what enhanced her face and figure. 'My whole life changed with Calvin', Kelly told Ingrid Sischy. Their affair began as an office romance. 'He would walk into the room and it was just like the lights went on … I was so much more special when he came into the room.' John Calcagno, one of Klein's designers, witnessed it first hand, comparing it to 'some kind of magic. He fell in love with her and she madly with him.'

Kelly wasn't a diva. She knew how to behave, never made public scenes and was independent, and that suited her older husband. As a couple, they seemed charmed. 'When they show up at a gala and the flashbulbs go overtime, observers could be forgiven for thinking that they, and not the Clintons, are the real heirs to Camelot', wrote Lisa Armstrong. 'They look glamorous because they are glamorous', Klein's friend Barry Diller told Armstrong. Christy Turlington described them as 'smart, stylish' and having a lot of fun together. 'Every American couple wants to be them', she enthused to Armstrong. Taking it further, Turlington offered that Klein 'should use her [Kelly] in his ads'.

Photographed by David Bailey in 1987, cover girl Christy Turlington wears a signature Klein look, described by Vogue as being 'a pearl white silk radzemire double-breasted shirt'.

***Overleaf** Turlington wears Klein's short camel-hair coat (left), described by Vogue as 'the new 7/8 swing proportion shorn of all detail' with polo-neck sweater and straw cavalry twill trousers with turn ups. Photography by Bill King, 1986. Photographed by Neil Kirk for Vogue's 'Manhattan Masterclass' feature in 1989 (right), Vanessa Duve wears Klein's cashmere cable knit polo-neck with matching scarf, beige wool gabardine jodhpurs, wool ankle socks and natural suede fur-lined ankle boots.*

VOGUE

NOV
£2·00

the new jackets

STRONG
DECORATIVE
DAY DRESSING

WHO GLITTERS?

fashion bravery

With a preference for faded jeans and an effortless simplicity that made her define 'the real, working woman', Kelly was described as 'Klein's marketing imagery made flesh'. A horse-y *Vogue* shoot with the top model Karen Mulder wearing Klein's clothes in 1991 was influenced by Kelly's 'clean outdoorsy style'. And the designer's promotion of the unitard in one collection was inspired by a Caribbean boat trip where his wife had worn one the whole time. Kelly also had an innate understanding of his clothes. One of Klein's renowned designs – the metallic lacy slip dress – looked as good on Kelly as it did on the style icon Bianca Jagger. Since the Kleins were both light-eyed, tanned and slim, it was hard not to agree with one observer that they made 'each other look fabulous'. And Armstrong made a lasting and valid point: 'Kelly seemed to be the catalyst Klein needed to make him look at the business and life from a fresh perspective.'

And Klein had to have freshness, always, saying, 'We need newness and excitement in fashion. That's what it's all about.' Via Kelly, he would channel a pure American classicism. It gave a needed breathing space in his work. His checking in to Hazelden had indicated that Klein was burnt out – creatively and emotionally. He trusted Kelly, and she kept him going and also kept track of the new fragrance, Eternity. There were those who complained that the house of Calvin Klein became too preppy, but Kelly's input kept it moving forwards. She was a muse who had worked in the designer's studio, understood his aims, but could also come up with new ideas. Importantly for the label's direction, it was Kelly who had said, 'there's something sexy about wearing your boyfriend's underwear'. She was a positive influence on her husband and he recognised it. 'What I'm doing now is absolutely about Kelly,' he told Armstrong in 1994, 'About how she works and loves life and leads an active one. She says things all the time that are inspirational to me.'

As an example of Vogue's 'Nineteen Deliciously Easy Pieces to Pack for Great Escapes' in 1992, Patrick Demarchelier photographed Tatjana Patitz wearing Klein's classic white jeans.

Overleaf *Described by Vogue as 'crystalline clarity in white', a smiling Linda Evangelista wears an 'Iridescent slash-necked short shift tapering to above-the-knee' (left). A signature Calvin Klein look, the design for Vogue Patterns is upbeat, timeless and well suited to the beach. Photograph by Patrick Demarchelier, 1990. A preppy look, captured by Eric Boman in 1992, sees Johanna Westin channelling a contemporary Grace Kelly (right), wearing Klein's silk georgette shirt and stone wool crêpe skirt that Vogue described as 'elegant [and] longer.'*

Klein was a control freak, a perfectionist and Kelly had the confidence to laugh good-naturedly at him or roll her eyes. When being interviewed by Armstrong, the designer admitted that 'the wrong thing in the wrong place or superfluous details' could still drive him nuts. 'I like things to be stripped back to their essentials, to a kind of purity', he said and then fixed his eyes on a droopy arrangement of roses and orchids that had just been sent to his wife. 'They're a very kind thought', he offered. 'But they're not my idea of how this place should look. I have a thing about wanting my surroundings to be a certain way. I strive for a certain kind of perfection.' It was the sort of behaviour that only a certain type could take but the calm-under-fire Kelly wasn't easily stirred. 'I have my own taste and it isn't always the same as his', she told Armstrong. 'But you know what? It's much better that way.'

Photographed by Snowdon for Vogue, *Calvin and Kelly stand on their jetty at low tide. Both in full evening regalia, Kelly wears one of Klein's simply cut but eye-catching gold lace evening dresses.*

Overleaf *In an image that resembles a lifestyle ad, Snowden shoots Calvin and Kelly wearing shirt, trousers and towelling robe from Calvin Klein's CK collection.*

In order to capture the Kleins' idyllic lifestyle, *Vogue* commissioned Lord Snowdon to illustrate Eve MacSweeney's article 'From Eternity to Here' in 1992. Picture after picture show a couple who are at ease and having fun. The first portrait has them lying on the sand with the crashing waves behind them. Wearing a denim shirt and khaki trousers, Klein holds his wife in his arms; she is wrapped in a golden brown towelling robe that matches her tanned limbs. Smiling at him, she's all hair, eyebrows and bright white teeth. The next page has the sphinx-like Mrs Klein sitting in the entrance hall. Wearing a green bodystocking, it emphasises her eyes and makes her look otherworldly. In the stables, sporting a T-shirt and chaps on his jeans, Klein looks perhaps a little out of place in comparison with his wife, who's wearing a white shirt, suede chaps and leather gloves. However, when kayaking on the nearby Georgica Pond, they seem as if they are genuinely relaxing. He looks comfortable in his tweed jacket and jeans while she resembles a wholesome college student in a ribbed golden brown cashmere tunic with matching leggings. Then there is a *Great Gatsby* shot with Klein wearing tails and his barefoot wife leaning against him in a gold lacy evening gown.

Their new home was built in the 1930s and was in such a state of disrepair that the Kleins commissioned Thierry Despont, the French architect, to rebuild it. In recreating authenticity for what he calls 'really just a simple, East Hampton shingle house', MacSweeney described the designer as demonstrating the 'all the obsessiveness that has kept him in such tight control of his much-franchised and licensed business.' 'The architect … I think I drove him crazy', Klein deadpanned. 'Every detail – every column, every shape, every curve – I would question him on.' The rooms were created to be spacious and well proportioned, with large windows and decks on all sides.

The décor's colour came via artwork such as the Georgia O'Keeffe pastel hanging above the massive stone hearth or one of Kelly's antique crosses punctuating the white walls. The bare floors were laid with broad, dark-stained boards that were brought in from old chapels and other buildings. Klein's chief fear was that the place would end up 'looking new, not lived in', whereas his goal was to be comfortable and give an impression that they belonged. Instead of talking about his individual belongings such as the set of seven chenille Aubusson deckchairs, Klein was keener to highlight the general ambience. 'It's about the simplicity of those floors and the strength of those wide planks', he said. 'Everything else is just basically white and view.'

For a 1992 Vogue feature entitled 'Plain and Beautiful', Arthur Elgort photographs Christy Turlington as a Golden-Age Hollywood actress on safari. For afternoon tea, she wears Klein's white side-split sundress with shoestring straps. An ideal look for the heat, its simple lines reinforce the designer's reputation as 'King of Clean'.

'What I do is make clothes that are personal, quiet, sexy and modern.'

CALVIN KLEIN

The interior perfectly exemplified Calvin Klein design. Yet the Kleins described it to Armstrong as 'a soothing, private bolt hole'. 'Like other American fashion giants – Donna Karan and Ralph Lauren are obvious comparisons –', Armstrong wrote, 'they are shrewd enough to know that every element of their lifestyle is a vital marketing tool'. Their beach home was a controlled environment where everything and everyone complemented each other – to such an extent that Armstrong quoted one observer as viewing it as 'a very subtle form of brainwashing' and almost rewriting life 'the way you'd like it to be'.

'At times, the seamless meshing of reality with image that has so distinguished Klein's persona', Armstrong wrote, 'has led to sections of the media to doubt the sincerity of some of his life changes. There have been accusations that he has recast his character or airbrushed his image every decade or so to mix 'n' match with the current zeitgeist.' When she broached this with Klein, he responded: 'If there's a rumour mill about my life, so be it,' he replied. 'I've never deliberately set out to be controversial or to capture the prevailing mood of a particular time. What I do is make clothes that are personal, quiet, sexy and modern.'

Klein's clothes weren't always 'quiet'. Nevertheless, throughout his career, Klein's designs can be seen to mirror his lifestyle and mood. Initially he made his reputation with a sporty style injected with sensuality. Then he became racier during the Studio 54 years before delving into the sophisticated – occasionally borrowing ideas from Yves Saint Laurent – and then becoming more conservative before evolving into classicism.

Demonstrating Klein's assured way with fabric, Naomi Campbell offers exotic allure in Klein's silk taffeta loose shirt, lightly gathered web lace skirt with elasticated waist, scalloped hem and crêpe-de-Chine underskirt. Photographed for Vogue's 'Winter Heat' feature by Patrick Demarchelier, 1988.

'We need newness and excitement in fashion.
That's what it's all about.'

CALVIN KLEIN

Whatever the motivation for his lifestyle changes, Klein was in the business of delivering dreams and to make them authentic he needed to live them, even if the period in question was short-lived. Besides, for most of his customers, he and his beautiful wife were indeed leading a dreamlike existence. When opening up to American *Vogue*'s Alessandra Stanley about Escape, his new fragrance in 1992, he naturally referred to Kelly and himself. Meanwhile, she described his married life as forging 'a passion for the aesthetics of the riding set, English antiques, club chairs purchased in Paris, Georgian silver', as well as discovering 'the good life: active, outdoors, away from it all'.

Claudia Mason wears Klein's signature shift dress for Vogue Patterns, made of sage satin-backed silk crêpe. Deceptively simple in design, its understated elegance is both smart and feminine. Photograph by Andrea Blanch, 1992.

The only mild bone of contention between the couple was Klein's need for minimalism. 'I keep putting things away and Kelly keeps bringing them out', he told Stanley. The second Mrs Klein had managed to coax him into allowing 'a few carefully placed bibelots – such as the thick Georgian pieces she loves – around the house'. In the opinion of Bloomingdale's Kal Ruttenstein, Kelly had managed to influence both the designer and the man. 'He absolutely defers to her, he is very interested in what she has to say about clothes and how people live … She has settled him down.' He added, 'I've never seen him happier or calmer.'

Thanks to Kelly, Klein had eased up on his schedule. 'He is really trying to find a more equal balance between work and play', Bruce Weber told Stanley. Having taken the photographs for Escape's ad campaign, Weber defined the fragrance's message as 'getting out, being active, finding things in your life that transport you in a really healthy way'.

'A woman on Wall Street doesn't want
to sit in a boardroom and have
everyone notice her dress.'

CALVIN KLEIN

The Klein marriage would last from 1986 to 1996. It was a significant decade for the designer. After the wildness of the 1970s and 1980s, he needed to unwind, take time for contemplation, to relax, and Kelly helped him do that. Her presence gave him focus and tranquillity. Of course, there were cynics who claimed it was a *mariage blanc* (a fake marriage), but it was a real relationship. There was a respect between the two. They were both attracted to each other. 'She is so Calvin, the image of what Calvin loves – American and clean and kind and beautiful', Diane von Furstenberg told Stanley. 'She is very much a reflection of him.' And when their relationship finally ended, they remained on good terms.

Kelly encouraged Klein to be more sporty and adventurous. For a husband suffering from addiction problems, it was an excellent idea – encouraging the natural high gleaned from adrenaline as opposed to that from booze and Valium. She bought him a Barnstable Cat – a small boat – and it led to the designer using bobbing sailing boats in the Escape ads, while the models in his shows began wearing minimal make-up, giving the impression that they had walked straight off a beach. Klein found peace of mind, sitting by the sea. And it's difficult not to feel that Kelly was responsible for helping her husband ease into the 1990s, a decade that he predicted to *Vogue* would be 'about the personal, about staying in and being alone and not flaunting what you have on your back or even in your driveway, but in your home, "the core of modern life" where people you love can share your investment.'

To celebrate the 1991 Diamond Jubilee edition of British Vogue, *75 designers were asked to make a one-off outfit. Klein designed 'a silver bugle beaded slip dress', a glamorous version of one of his signature styles. Photographed by Sheila Metzner, it was worn by Josie Borain who was the model for his original Obsession campaign.*

'Often the goal is to be inventive, creative, on the edge ... and sometimes provocative and sexy.'

CALVIN KLEIN

'EVERYBODY ALWAYS DOES
WHAT CALVIN DOES.'

VOGUE

STYLE THAT LASTS

In 1992, Calvin Klein's company almost crashed when the designer-jeans market collapsed. 'I took my daughter for a walk on the beach in the Hamptons', the designer would later admit, 'and said, we might have to sell everything.' Luckily, Klein's friend David Geffen stepped in and bailed out the company by buying the huge junk-bond debt ($62 million in face value). Then Citicorp, in a strong vote of confidence in the company, lent Klein the money to buy back Geffen's bonds, which he did, netting Geffen a handsome profit. The shock and drama required Klein to reassess his company. 'I may have gotten complacent', Klein told *Vanity Fair*. 'We think things are good and all of a sudden you turn around and it falls apart.' Yet oddly enough the terrifying incident was the needed spark for his re-renaissance as a designer.

When relaunching his Obsession fragrance in 1993, Calvin Klein chose the young Kate Moss, and had her photographed by Mario Sorrenti, her Italian boyfriend. Recognising a new wave in fashion, he immediately understood that she would become a mega model, viewing her as the 1990s' version of Jean Shrimpton.

In 1993, on the advice of his daughter Marci, he entered the bridge, or lower-price point, category with CK Calvin Klein women's apparel. Marci had complained that his clothes were too expensive and not cutting edge enough for either her or her generation. When he presented his lower-priced and youth-orientated line, which featured a hip mix of crinkled cotton shirt, a leather butcher-apron dress, oversized men's jackets, lean trousers and a jean jacket cut with tails, it was an instant success. Hailed by Amy Spindler, the *New York Times*'s critic, it captured 'everything exciting in street-level fashion'. The styles also fitted with Klein's prediction to *Vogue* that there was 'going to be a big change in the Nineties', that it would be 'more liberal, more free and maybe more exciting'. 'It's less about flash', he said, 'and more about people in the streets, the environment.'

There was also his new professional crush on the model Kate Moss. Klein had always admired English women's attitude to fashion. In the late 1980s, he had hired Grace Coddington – one of British *Vogue*'s legendary fashion editors – to style his collection and when she left to join Anna Wintour at American *Vogue*, Polly Hamilton, another British *Vogue* stylist, would eventually replace her.

In 1992 Klein turned Kate Moss into a household name with a series of underwear ads featuring her topless with the then-rapper 'Marky Mark' Wahlberg and the slogan: 'The best protection against AIDS is to keep your Calvins on.' Wrapped around Wahlberg, Moss with her heart-shaped face and bee-stung lips was yet another *femme-enfant*, reminiscent of Brooke Shields but with fewer clothes. Klein responded to her air of innocence combined with an element of the naughty schoolgirl from the wrong side of the tracks.

The photographer Mario Sorrenti was Moss's boyfriend at the time, and it was after seeing Sorrenti's private pictures of Moss that Klein decided to use her for the relaunch of Obsession for Men. The designer's challenge for the campaign was rejuvenating the campaign and bringing it into the Nineties. The best way was making the obsession real and personal. Klein found this when going through Sorrenti's work. 'I said, he's really obsessed with her, he's passionate for her, it's all so clear. And it's fresh, and it's young, and it's new.'

The series of portraits by taken by Sorrenti included Moss lying on a sofa, her tiny behind exposed, and another of her topless with her spindly fingers suggestively touching her mouth. Dubbing her the queen of the waifs, the campaign caused an uproar in the US. Critics accused her of being unshapely and even borderline anorexic. Klein disagreed. 'I see Kate Moss on the buses all over the country', he told *Women's Wear Daily*. 'And I think it's the sexiest goddamn shot I've done in I can't tell you how long.'

For Vogue's *'Big-City Bright Lights' portfolio of people illuminating London in 1993, Andrew Macpherson photographed the 19-year-old Kate Moss wearing Calvin Klein's singlet with her boyfriend, the 21-year-old photographer Mario Sorrenti. It was their relationship – they were living together, enjoying a bohemian existence in Notting Hill – that inspired Klein's decision to hire both Moss and Sorrenti.*

'Everyone in Calvin's world was gorgeous. Sexy. Sensual … The imagery that he used to communicate that changed the worlds of fashion and advertising.'

MARC JACOBS

Moss's unaffected straightforwardness appealed. 'A lot of women were getting implants and doing things to their buttocks', Klein said later. 'It was out of control. I just found something so distasteful about all that. I wanted someone who was natural, always thin. I was looking for the complete opposite of the glamour type before Kate.'

Enchanted by Moss and viewing her as the Jean Shrimpton of her time, he was also won over by her rock'n'roll style and fondness for vintage shops. In fact, her choice of knee-length vintage dresses would inspire the hem length of Klein's groundbreaking 1994 autumn/winter collection. 'There's something very sexy about suddenly seeing more of the leg covered up', he told American *Vogue*'s Julia Reed. 'And then seeing the leg in sheer hose or naked, as opposed to very short skirts with tights in a matching colour.' It was something quite different; in spite of a few editors insisting that it was 'dowdy', the length became a sell-out and would inspire the following season. Reed was not surprised. 'Everybody always does what Calvin does', she declared. 'He made tighter jeans and charged twice as much, sold 200,000 pairs the next week … He decided it would be sexy to put women into men's briefs and forced Jockey to play catch-up with its own product. He sent favourite Seventies models Patti Hansen and Rosie Vela down his runway last season, and within a year they were appearing in ads for major cosmetic companies … More than anything, he knows fashion is about change, and with barely a flick of the wrist and about four inches, he has moved fashion another step forward.'

Nadja Auermann wears Klein's wool-mix knee-length classic shift dress. 'Fussy is out, simple is in', wrote Vogue, calling it 'The New Chic'. 'Cool in camel: the newest neutral, whether it colours a shirt, jacket or coat, flatters even the palest skin.' Photograph by Jacques Olivar, 1995.

'I'm not doing costumes. I'm doing very real clothes for the modern woman.'

CALVIN KLEIN

Reed described the mid-90s as Klein's moment. 'He has triumphed as the womenswear and menswear designer of the year… sold his controversial underwear line for a fortune and is ready to launch yet another mega-fragrance', she continued.

Klein became a steady, constantly quoted voice throughout the pages of *Vogue*. In a 1993 article called 'Independent's Day', described as talking to 'the talents shaping fashion', Katherine Betts wrote: 'This season … nine designers stand head and shoulder above the fray.' Naturally, Klein was included, with emphasis on the fact that he sent women of all ages down his catwalk, from the 49-year-old Lauren Hutton to 19-year-old Kate Moss. 'Fashion isn't about age anymore, it's about an attitude', Klein said. Nor was it about distinguishing between day and evening clothes. And he had dared to do away with 'complicated layers and accessories'. 'I've been mixing and layering and doing all these subtle combination of textures and patterns', he said. 'But I'm tired of all that. I want to focus on my purity and ease of dressing. It's about minimalism, very strong and very modern.' A black-and-white photograph accompanied the piece showing middle-aged models such as Patti Hansen and Lauren Hutton looking stylish and fooling around with younger ones such as Linda Evangelista, Kristen McMenamy and Lucie de la Falaise.

'Thirties-inspired bias cutting and elegant long lines, evening wear revisits Hollywood glamour', wrote Vogue of Klein's flowing silk satin dress, worn by Carolyn Murphy and photographed by Regan Cameron for Vogue's 'Siren Call' feature in 2002.

Klein's 'stroke of genius' in using mature models had come about after having dinner with Lisa Taylor, the supermodel of the 1970s. 'He had taken her out for her thirtieth birthday, and he hadn't seen her in years', wrote Julia Reed. 'And she called and said she was in New York and she'd just turned 40.' During dinner, Klein began looking at her and thinking, 'my god, you know, how is that I have never noticed before how amazing women are at the age of 40? And I, I always used to have a thing for her. She's so sexy. And I thought, Jesus, she's gotten every sexier because she's now like a real woman, she's no kid.'

He asked her if she would 'consider taking some photographs' and then got the photographer Steven Meisel involved. Taylor had starred in Helmut Newton's notorious 1975 photograph (shown here on page 42) that still looks so modern, wrote Reed 'that the picture could easily have been taken today.' 'In an era when women were coming into their own, he [Klein] understood them', offered Reed. Much of it was to do with respect: allowing them to be active and strong, and yet look feminine and sensual.

To illustrate Vogue's 'Long Hot Summer Evenings', Claudia Mason wears Klein's silk organza tunic, slit up both sides, over washed-silk organza flared trousers. 'Body shape is important', wrote Vogue, 'even when it doesn't define the silhouette [and is] hazily visible through sheer fabrics'. Photograph by Sante d'Orazio, 1993.

***Overleaf** Naomi Campbell in Klein's easy stretch separates: a rayon strappy top and washed silk fitted skirt demonstrating Klein's 'new clarity of colour'. 'Uncomplicated urban dressing has lost all overtones of executive aggression', enthused Vogue. 'Gentle lines caress the body ... for a look of effortless assurance.' Photograph by Arthur Elgort, 1989.*

This was six years after Klein had opened his first British shop at Harvey Nichols in 1988. 'The style I believe in is one that lasts', Klein told *Vogue*'s Sarah Mower who viewed his clothes being made for grown-up women who 'needed to dress with minimum fuss and maximum impact'. Famous as Klein was in America, he was still relatively unknown in Europe. However, he had felt that European women had changed or rather outgrown the ideal of being decorative or fussy, of being 'pretty for the man'. 'Now', he told Reed in 1994, 'they want to dress like American women. They want to wear flats. And so what I'm doing, my style, which is about purity and simplicity and less is more, has appeal all over the world.'

Reed discovered that Klein thought 'about clothes all the time', lived and breathed his business and possessed a democratic sensibility and playful attitude. 'The change aspect of fashion is what is really so exciting, because it's fun', he said. 'When I started doing the underwear, for example, for very little money, men could suddenly have some fun. I mean, you can take something that everyone has always thought of as being not very interesting and just something that you need and turn it into something that could be fun, that could be sexy, that could be different.'

'I want to focus on my purity and ease of dressing.'

CALVIN KLEIN

'I ALWAYS WANTED THE FABRICS TO FEEL SEXY ON A WOMAN'S BODY.'

CALVIN KLEIN

In Klein's seasoned opinion, there were so many 'ideas and styles and approaches' that could be attached to 'something basic'. 'And for not a lot of money, people can get enjoyment out of it. Fashion should be like that.' Regarding those who were 'wealthy enough to afford the clothes', it was 'another kind of fun' that he described as 'luxurious and very rarefied'.

Klein, albeit a self-proclaimed control freak, was not a fashion dictator and had no problems with his customers cutting his skirt length. 'It's very easy', he told *Vogue*. 'I put clothes on the runway, and I do hair and makeup and a shoe with the dress or the suit or whatever it is. And I'm saying this is what I think is the newest of me and the most interesting. And you don't have to wear it quite like that if you don't want to. I mean it's a wonderful thing. People have choices.'

American *Vogue* called CK One – his first unisex fragrance – 'his latest exercise in democracy'. Costing $50, its flat screw-top container was stylish yet solid because, in his experience, men didn't like 'pretty little bottle things' and was the type of scent to be splashed on heartily. 'It's what I've always liked', Klein said. 'It comes from the idea of men and women sharing things.' He also believed that women like to use a man's fragrance. 'Men put on a lot of stuff', he continued, 'and there's something very sexy if the scent is so light and so fresh and so masculine and you can put a lot on. I mean when a woman does that, as long as it's not overbearing, it's very sexy.'

The campaign for CK One was fairly gritty, channelling Richard Avedon's black-and-white portraits, taken in the late Sixties, of

*In 'The New Rules of Short',
Vogue declared that
'Calvin Klein's biker boots
bring the simplest of shifts
bang up to date.' This was
well illustrated by Angela
Lindvall's rangy frame in
Klein's Nappa shearling
dress and leather boots.
Photograph by Thomas
Schenk, 2001.*

*Previous pages Klein's
crêpe A-line tunic and
hipsters in 'colour blinding'
orange, worn by Stella
Tennant (left), are described
by Vogue as bringing
'new life to this summer's
slender, simple silhouette'.
Photograph by Arthur
Elgort, 1996.
Jeurgen Teller captures
Linda Evangelista wearing
Klein's tailored wool crêpe
jacket (right) accentuating
her curves. 'In black, it's
the epitome of today's sleek
chic', said Vogue in 1994.*

'It's about minimalism, very strong
and very modern.'

CALVIN KLEIN

Andy Warhol and his factory members. Photographed by Steven Meisel, it used young members of Hollywood, such as Sofia Coppola, and dozens of models, such as Moss, posing as ordinary people. With an aim to take the campaign to the streets, the images were posted on outdoor venues such as billboards and bus shelters.

In 1995, the designer did an about turn, sending out a collection that American *Vogue*'s Katherine Betts deemed 'classic, clean-cut and conservative', and was inspired by style icons of the 1950s. 'Backstage at the Calvin Klein show', she wrote, 'Kate Moss, of dressed-down Nineties style, is carefully fixing her chignon and adjusting the jacket of her slightly dowdy camel suit while Klein waxes on about the timeless elegance of Audrey Hepburn and Grace Kelly.' Klein was always at his effortless best when spare and understated, as was illustrated by a satin slip dress – a timeless classic that spanned generations, looking superb on his wife Kelly and on Winona Ryder when depicted on the cover of American *Vogue*. This style obviously contrasted with his disastrous attempt at monastic chic in 1993 when he had sent out models in long priest coats and shapeless velvet dresses.

O nce a chic simplicity returned to fashion (promoted by the meteoric rise of the Austrian designer Helmut Lang) Klein was in his element, since he knew how to balance sportswear with simple refinement and a sprinkle of street credibility and edginess. 'If Calvin Klein's CK One ads or Gianni Versace's couture ads are any indication', wrote Betts in 1996 under the heading of 'The Neo-Modernists', 'the minimal, almost generic look of the Neo-modernist is already migrating through the fashion system.'

Mimi Anden wears Klein's fresh and simple white cotton trouser suit (left) in his spring/summer 'Black and White' show of 2001, which Vogue described as having a 'sexy silhouette'. Photograph by Roger Dean. In the same show, supermodel Gisele Bündchen (right) in Klein's edgy, silky slip dress.

Overleaf *Mikael Jansson photographs Caroline de Maigret in Klein's chic crêpe sleeveless dress (left). As if describing Klein's designs, the theme of the shoot in 1994 was 'clothes a woman rarely tires of' and 'key wardrobe pieces'. Photographed by Nick Knight in 1997 (right), Vogue's cover girl Amber Valletta is appealingly 'strong and sexy' in Klein's crêpe and gauze sleeveless slip dress.*

'He was the first to understand
how to say more with less.'

VOGUE

VOGUE

JUNE
£2.80

HOLLYWOOD UNZIPPED
style secrets
at the Oscars

Do health
foods really
work?

**STRONG
AND SEXY**
the best looks for
beach and gym

GURU GUIDE
who follows who

LOOKING GOOD
beauty and fitness special

'In these ads, what they're wearing is almost irrelevant. What you notice first is the model's attitude ...' As Klein had previously predicted, fashion had become about attitude.

Photographer Kelly Klein, the designer's former wife, captures Gisele Bündchen in Klein's minimalist cotton tank and artfully cut sarong skirt, in 1998.

Overleaf The actor and rapper Mark Wahlberg, star of Calvin Klein's early underwear ads, wears Klein's Y-fronts and jeans, exaggeratedly low-slung (left), on the runway at the Seventh Annual California Fashion Industry Friends of AIDS Project Los Angeles. The 1993 benefit dinner and show, at the Hollywood Bowl, were held in Klein's honour. Alek Wek flexes her muscles for Arthur Elgort (right) in Vogue's 'Power Cuts' shoot in 1997. The magazine recommended 'streamlined pieces in flexible fabrics' as illustrated by Klein's sportswear ensemble of cotton and lycra top and leggings.

He was also in step with Bett's 1998 *Vogue* article called 'Rumblings in the Rank' that compared his company, along with Ralph Lauren and Donna Karan, to the big commercial film studios whereas, for example, Comme des Garçons' Rei Kawabuko was analogous to an 'indie' filmmaker. In Betts's opinion 'instead of competing with one another, super established names like Chanel, Giorgio Armani, Calvin Klein and Miuccia Prada have to compete with the logos that dominate the mass media: Nike, Coca-Cola, Disney and Apple.' She stated that 'People now compare Ralph Lauren to Coca-Cola rather than to John Galliano.' It was a valid albeit depressing outlook on the fashion world. She noted, however, that Klein, like Lauren, reached 'beyond Seventh Avenue' via 'shoes, watches and sheets with furniture and rugs coming'.

In the same year, in 'Smart Thinking', an article for British V*ogue*, Suzy Menkes questioned Klein for 'following the intellectual path' (and expressed her dismay when he strayed away from his clean lines to complicate 'his simple silhouettes with drawstrings and smocking'). Klein had, after all, made his reputation 'with simple, user friendly clothes'. Menkes had a valid point. Klein's talent was always unsurpassed when left streamlined: that was how he made his mark in fashion.

'The style I believe in is one that lasts.'

CALVIN KLEIN

'CALVIN'S
CLOTHING SEEMED
TO BE ALL ABOUT
THE SENSATION
OF TOUCH AND
THE PROVOCATION
OF GETTING NAKED.'

MARC JACOBS

Calvin Klein photographed
for Vogue by Marc Hom
in 1997. The easy
androgynous style of his
sharply cut staples such
as coat and trousers is
enduring and ageless.

Previous page For Vogue's
'Spa Guide', Pamela Hanson
shows Eva Herzigová in
1998 sporting Klein's bikini
in a wrap-around design
that is both sexy and chic.

A purist, he was best when unpretentious as demonstrated by a soft silk blouse with matching skirt, a classic dress with cap sleeves, a slouchy trouser suit and a long silk slip dress. He also achieved enormous success with simple yet innovative ideas: designer jeans and boyish underwear were deceptively straightforward. To appreciate his marketing genius, his flair lay both in his natural understanding of the times he lived in and in his ability to bring sex into advertising in a pioneering way. No hypocrite, he was unembarrassed by his sensual side, so his use of it in his work was regarded as authentic and therefore tolerated.

As for his personal life, it was compartmentalised. He was a devoted father, a fascinating and generous husband but someone who was sexually ambiguous. His erotic adventures had been considerable but had never quite left him satisfied. The same applied to his substance abuse. By his own admission, Klein was an addict, but a functioning one who, despite his failings, had achieved miracles in the fashion industry.

In 2003, he and Barry Schwartz sold the company to Phillips-Van Heusen for a deal worth over $700 million. Others might have enjoyed this fortune gracefully, but Klein blew it all by then having a public, highly visible, match-interrupting meltdown at a New York Knicks game in Manhattan's Madison Square Garden. However, yet again, the public seemed to view it as the illustrious designer showing his human side – the King of Clean was flawed yet fantastic.

Or as he admitted: 'I have a gift. I get an emotional reaction.' It was with this 'emotional reaction' that he continued to produce winning new designs right until he finally relinquished control of his company. A crisp blue cotton shirt dress; a flecked heather cashmere crew neck; a white trouser suit; a distressed leather jacket and a loose satin top with a panelled skirt; all produced in the early years of the millennium, each one held to be a perfect example of its kind. As he said: 'Fashion is about change. It has to be new. You have to keep pushing it.'

Index

Page numbers in *italic* refer to illustrations

References

Gaines, Steven and Sharon Churcher Obsession: The Lives and Times of Calvin Klein,
Carol Publishing Group 1994

Marsh, Lisa The House of Klein: Fashion, Controversy and a Business Obsession,
John Wiley & Sons Inc., 2003

Pigozzi, Jean C Pigozzi's Journal of the Seventies, Doubleday, Dolphin, 1979

Picture credits

All photographs © The Condé Nast Publications Ltd except the following:

4 Parkerphotography / Alamy Stock Photo; 12 Pierre / Rex / Shutterstock; 24 Gianni Penati / Vogue © Condé Nast Inc 1971; 26 Francesco Scavullo / Vogue © Condé Nast Inc 1974; 29 Francesco Scavullo / Vogue © Condé Nast Inc 1974; 30-31 Bernard Gotfryd / Getty Images; 36-37 Duane Michals / Vogue © Condé Nast Inc 1975; 41 Arthur Elgort / Vogue © Condé Nast Inc 1976; 42 © Helmut Newton Estate; 44 Arthur Elgort / Vogue © Condé Nast Inc 1977; 47 Arthur Elgort / Vogue © Condé Nast Inc 1977; 48-49 Oliviero Toscani / Vogue © Condé Nast Inc 1977; 50 Bettmann / Getty Images; 61 Waring Abbott / Getty Images; 65 Bettmann / Getty Images; 66-67 © Bruce Weber; 83 Rex / Shutterstock; 99 Ron Galella / Wireimage / Getty Images; 128 Pictorial Press / Alamy Stock Photo; 141 © Juergen Teller; 145 Victor Virgile / Gamma-Rapho via Getty Images; 150 Ron Galella /Wireimage / Getty Images.

Back Cover REX / Shutterstock

Acknowledgements

Once again, I have to thank Alexandra Shulman and Harriet Wilson as well as Quadrille's Jane O'Shea. Calvin Klein remains one of the most talented and charismatic designers in the history of American fashion. With his aim to surprise and compel each season, I became indebted to excellent articles penned by esteemed *Vogue* writers such as Lisa Armstrong, Katherine Betts, Eve MacSweeney, Suzy Menkes, Sarah Mower, Maureen Orth, Julia Reed and Alessandra Stanley. Mention must also be made of the late Ingrid Sischy and her superb Calvin Klein profile, written for *Vanity Fair* in 2008. *Vogue* image and article research was greatly eased by Brett Croft, Condé Nast's Archive Manager, Sarah Brown and Poppy Roy. Concerning the names of models – essential to Klein's reputation – I relied on the expertise of Dior's Jerome Gautier. At Quadrille, a leader in art and photography, I was in constant contact with Nicola Ellis and Gemma Hayden. For a second time, I relied on the editing skills of Sarah Mitchell who was her tactful and encouraging self. The latter also applies to my agents Ed Victor and Maggie Phillips.

Finally, Calvin Klein took delight in empowering women. It's a tradition that continues in the pages of *Vogue*.

Publishing Consultant Jane O'Shea
Creative Director Helen Lewis
Series Editor Sarah Mitchell
Series Designer Nicola Ellis
Designer Gemma Hayden
Production Director Vincent Smith
Production Controller Emily Noto

For *Vogue*:
Commissioning Editor Harriet Wilson
Picture Researchers Sarah Brown
                    Poppy Roy

First published in 2017 by
Quadrille Publishing Limited
Pentagon House
52-54 Southwark Street
London SE1 1UN
www.quadrille.co.uk

Text copyright © 2017 Condé Nast
Publications Limited
Vogue Regd TM is owned by the Condé
Nast Publications Ltd and is used under
licence from it. All rights reserved.

Design and layout © 2017 Quadrille
Publishing Limited

Quadrille is an imprint of Hardie Grant
www.hardiegrant.com.au

All rights reserved. No part of this book
may be reproduced, stored in a retrieval
system or transmitted in any form or
by any means, electronic, electrostatic,
magnetic tape, mechanical, photocopying,
recording or otherwise, without the prior
permission in writing of the publisher.

The rights of Natasha Fraser-Cavassoni
to be identified as the author of this work
have been asserted by her in accordance
with the Copyright, Design and Patents
Act 1988.

Cataloguing in Publication Data: a
catalogue record for this book is
available from the British Library.

ISBN 978 184949 970 5

Printed in China